HOW DID
EVIL
COME INTO THE WORLD?

CHRISTIAN ANSWERS TO HARD QUESTIONS

Christian Interpretations of Genesis 1

Christianity and the Role of Philosophy

Creation, Evolution, and Intelligent Design

Did Adam Exist?

How Can I Know for Sure?

How Did Evil Come into the World?

The Morality of God in the Old Testament

Should You Believe in God?

Was Jesus Really Born of a Virgin?

Peter A. Lillback and Steven T. Huff, Series Editors

HOW DID
EVIL
COME INTO THE WORLD?

WILLIAM EDGAR

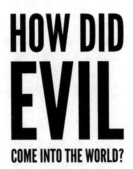

PHILADELPHIA, PENNSYLVANIA

PUBLISHING

P.O. BOX 817 • PHILLIPSBURG • NEW JERSEY 08865-0817

Westminster Seminary Press, LLC, a Pennsylvania limited liability company, is a wholly owned subsidiary of Westminster Theological Seminary.

This work is a co-publication of P&R Publishing and Westminster Seminary Press, LLC.

Scripture quotations are from *ESV Bible*® (*The Holy Bible, English Standard Version*®). Copyright © 2007 by Crossway Bibles, a publishing ministry of Good News Publishers. Used by permission. All rights reserved.

ISBN: 978-1-59638-671-6 (pbk)
ISBN: 978-1-59638-776-8 (ePub)
ISBN: 978-1-59638-777-5 (Mobi)

Printed in the United States of America

Library of Congress Cataloging-in-Publication Data

Edgar, William, 1944-
  How did evil come into the world? / William Edgar, Westminster Seminary Press, Philadelphia, Pennsylvania. -- 1st ed.
    pages cm. -- (Christian answers to hard questions)
  Includes bibliographical references.
  ISBN 978-1-59638-671-6 (pbk.)
  1. Good and evil--Biblical teaching. 2. Eden. 3. Adam (Biblical figure) 4. Eve (Biblical figure) I. Title.
  BS680.G6E34 2014
  231'.8--dc23
                          2013042616

SIMPLY STATED, in our world things are not the way they are supposed to be.[1] One would have to be living in a bubble not to know that. A tsunami wipes out millions of people in the Pacific Ring of Fire. A child dies of leukemia. A famine overwhelms large parts of East Africa. A husband abuses his wife. Warlords prowl the hills of Afghanistan. A gunman enters an elementary school and murders scores of students and teachers. Yet evil does not have to be so dramatic to qualify as evil. Tarring a reputation by gossip, adjusting the figures on one's income tax, glancing lustfully at the opposite sex—these are not the way things are supposed to be either.

Finally, even though everything in us cries out for life, everyone, even the most privileged people, will ultimately have to face death, the great leveler. We sense profoundly that death is not natural or normal, as much as we try to whitewash it. Things are not the way they are supposed to be.

Natural disasters certainly qualify as evil, for they are often horribly destructive. So do famines, whether or not they are perpetrated by corrupt human beings. We will discuss those subjects. Yet surely the most devastating forms of evil come from human causes. Are human beings, then, the ultimate cause of evil? What if there is a God, one who is both good and all-powerful? Would he not somehow be ultimately responsible for evil? If so, how is he then still good? The question is: where does evil come from?

BEFORE WE MOVE ON

✚ What is the connection between a natural disaster and a human act of terrorism? Despite their differences, why might both indicate that things in the world are "not the way they are supposed to be"?

5

+ How would you define *evil*, working from the descriptions
  in these opening paragraphs?

+ What are some causes of evil? Are there different causes
  for different kinds of evil? Are there other possible causes
  that the author did not mention?

+ Where might the ultimate *responsibility* for the existence
  of evil lie? Why?

THINGS MIGHT HAVE BEEN DIFFERENT

There is no disputing that human beings cause evil. One of
the most powerful novels of the twentieth century was Albert
Camus's *The Fall*, set in a bar in Amsterdam. In the novel, Jean-
Baptiste Clamence confesses his life's story to a stranger. He had
been a prominent, respected defense lawyer in Paris. Always on the
side of the widow, always ready to help the poor, he had thought
of himself as a model human being, well above the average slob.
Until one night as he was walking home, crossing the Pont Neuf,
he spotted a woman leaning over the bridge. She was about to
take her life. He walked right by. He even heard the splash, a
struggle, and then . . . nothing. Why hadn't he helped her? Why
had he failed to intercede? As the story unfolds, Clamence tells of
other occasions when he lost nerve. Here he is now, a broken man,
in Amsterdam, telling a complete stranger about his sinfulness.
Amsterdam is cold, dark, dreary. Its canals run in circles, just like
the circles of Hell in Dante's immortal *Divine Comedy*.

Camus, not necessarily a Christian, had a profound sense
that we are in a fallen world and that we are all complicit in the
cowardly state that allows and even perpetrates evil. The heart
of this evil is deception, including self-deception. All of us are
involved. Camus is confessing for all of us. If there were no deception, think what our world would look like. The economy would

be stable. Spouses would not cheat on each other. Advertising would be honest. The very title of the book, *The Fall*, shows that Camus had some awareness of the abnormality of the world. A fall from what? When did it happen? Why are things so abnormal? Is there a scientific explanation? Does science have anything at all to say about this state of affairs, or do we rely solely on "religious" truth?

BEFORE WE MOVE ON

+ How do human beings cause and perpetuate evil? How is our complicity in evil the result of deception?

+ What does the story of Jean-Baptiste Clamence illustrate? In what sense is he "confessing for all of us"?

+ What do you think the world would look like without deception?

What about death itself? In what sense are human beings the cause of their own death? Here we need to draw back the curtain. Though it might seem incredible to us today, the biblical account of how things went wrong provides a convincing explanation for human causality, all the while showing us how the good, all-powerful God of the universe is somehow both in control and nevertheless innocent of the entrance of evil into our world.

BEFORE WE MOVE ON

+ What new claim is the author making? What does this mean about the ultimate responsibility for evil?

What is evil, anyway? Suffering is usually disagreeable and can be evil when it is caused by something that is wrong. So we would not call the sensation of being burned evil if it protects us from the fire. But it would be evil if we caused someone to be burned for malevolent purposes. The ultimate definition of evil is that it is against God. Put the other way, evil is what God is against. On almost every page of Scripture we are told that God opposes evil—indeed, that he is outraged by it. Habbakuk describes him this way: "You who are of purer eyes than to see evil and cannot look at wrong" (Hab. 1:13). "Ah, sinful nation," God calls Israel, "a people laden with iniquity" (Isa. 1:4). The idea of blaming God for evil is repulsive to the authors of Scripture. "Let no one say when he is tempted, 'I am being tempted by God,' for God cannot be tempted with evil, and he himself tempts no one" (James 1:13). Indeed, God is "the Father of lights with whom there is no variation or shadow due to change" (1:17). So then, if God is God, how did evil come into the world?

Before we move on

+ What is the author's definition of *evil*? How does it compare to your own definition from earlier? How does it encompass the different examples of evil given at the start of the booklet?

The Bible teaches very insistently that there was a before and an after. In the earliest pages of Genesis, we read that God made the world good. Following the grand description of the creation week, the first chapter of Genesis concludes this way: "And God saw everything that he had made, and behold, it was very good" (Gen. 1:31). The crown of God's creation is mankind, made after his own image, made male and female (1:26–27). The great calling of humanity is to multiply, to spread over the earth, and to rule over it for God's sake (1:28–30). Everything was good and right. Adam and Eve were placed in a gorgeous garden and told to take care of it. In the ancient world, kings and queens often had beautiful gardens around them to signify their royalty.

This account becomes more intriguing. The Lord God placed our first parents, particularly Adam, in a special role. He was to represent the entire human race and set the direction for its future. Why such an arrangement? Because God wanted humanity to be united. To accomplish such a solidarity, he set them in a covenant relation to their head. A covenant is an arrangement whereby God enters into a contract with his people. No analogy is perfect. But it is something like subjects' being united through their king, or tribe members' being united through the chief. In this case, our human fellowship in the covenant is an earthly reflection of the way that God himself relates to the entire creation as its covenant head.

With such an arrangement characterizing humanity through its head, God gave our first parents an opportunity to grow into greater maturity and to become even happier than they were. In doing so, he set the stakes high. For Adam and Eve were responsible not only for their own futures, but for the future of all humanity. God put them to a test, telling them to resist eating of the fruit from the tree of the knowledge of good and evil. Everything else was permitted, but not that tree. Take that fruit, and you die (Gen. 2:16–17). Resist, and you grow and grow until you attain eternal life.

Why such a test? For one thing, it was God's way of showing this first couple who was in charge. Though he never ruled them harshly—quite the contrary—the Lord wanted human beings, with all the privileges they received, to remember where those privileges and gifts came from. For another, this was part of God's plan for the future. He wanted to bring mankind from the state of innocence in the garden to a state of fuller maturity, even of consummate bliss. According to the Bible, the way to achieve such maturity is both to learn, often through trials, to discern good and evil, and also to know how to resist evil (Deut. 1:39; 30:15; 2 Sam. 14:17; 1 Kings 3:9; etc.). Even Jesus, God's Son, had to learn good and evil through trials with respect to his humanity (Phil. 2:8; Heb. 5:8). Thus, *knowing* good and evil is more than an intellectual concept. It has to do with experience. Adam and Eve already knew the concept of evil: disobeying God would lead to death. But they could develop into a higher state of wisdom and growth only by experiencing and resisting the temptation to "be like God" (Gen. 3:5).

Before we move on

+ What is a *covenant head*? What are the benefits of having a covenant head?

+ Why would God test his creation? What were the benefits of passing the test?

+ What does it mean to know good and evil? How are good and evil known?

GOD'S PURPOSES

This might seem a strange story to us. Why such an apparently arbitrary test? And if the world was created good, how exactly did evil intrude? Why a talking serpent? We do not know all the details here. No doubt the serpent is the voice-piece of the Devil, in which case we must presume a fall in the invisible world. Even though it was originally created good, the invisible angelic world developed trouble sometime before Genesis 3. All we really know is that some angels were considered faithful and others were not (1 Tim. 5:21). For an Israelite reader, the serpent was a lowly, repugnant creature, one that represented the enemies of God himself (Job 26:13; Isa. 27:1). The serpent here is described as "crafty" (Gen. 3:1). The

Hebrew word is ambiguous, for it can mean "wise" or it can mean "wily." It is also a play on words, because it is almost identical to the word *naked* (3:7, 11). By trying to become wise or crafty in the wrong way, the man and the woman would know that they were naked, know that they had previously been fine, but realize that from now on they would be ashamed, exposed.

The test has meaning simply because God constructed it, not because there was some magic in the fruit. It is a test about allegiance, not about discerning whether one fruit is better than another. There was nothing special about that particular tree: though it may have been beautiful, it was not more attractive than other trees in the garden; nor was there something cursed about it. God could have picked any tree, or any other object. The tree did have a name, however: "the tree of the knowledge of good and evil" (Gen. 2:9). Those are good things. God had no objections to mankind's understanding good and evil. However, such knowledge had to be gained on his terms, not theirs. Here, it is by resisting the fruit and the voice of the serpent that our first parents could gain such knowledge. The point is, the man and woman were being tested as to whether they trusted God. Sadly, very sadly, they did not. Their progeny fell with them (a concept sometimes called *original sin*).

Before we move on

+ What was this test all about?
+ Why did Adam and Eve eat the forbidden fruit? What opportunities did they forfeit in doing so?

CONTOURS OF THE FALL

As a result, dreadful events occurred, spoiling all of this beautiful world. Our first parents, Adam and Eve, listened to the logic of a talking serpent and decided to trust that voice rather than the voice of God. The serpent tempted them by portraying God as jealous, selfish, and not wanting to share his knowledge with human beings. This could not have been further from the truth. God was happy to have mankind know about all kinds of things, including more about good and evil—not by disobedience, but by taking the right path. So when they took of that fruit, their eyes were indeed opened to good and evil, but in this case it was because they actually committed evil rather than resisting it. They knew evil, which could have been a good thing, yet they found out about it not by listening to God, but by succumbing to evil, and thus they lost everything. What exactly did they lose?

First, they became spiritually dead. That is, they lost their wonderful fellowship with God. Instead of walking with God in the cool of the day, they now hid from him in fear and had to hear those dreadful words: "What is this that you have done?" (Gen. 3:13). Second, they would indeed die physically as well. From this point on, all their descendants would die, both spiritually and physically. Third, every kind of relationship was corrupted. Human beings would fight and distrust one another, often resorting to a hatred leading to killing. Marriages would go sour. Childbearing would be painful. Proper authority would be questioned. And what was meant to be a gentle lordship over the creation would now be reversed, and the earth would reclaim us in death. Furthermore, according to the biblical account, the earth itself was cursed because of human disobedience (Gen. 3:17). Although in the midst of the curses God announced hope that all evil would finally be overcome, and although life would go on even in corruption, the misery of existence would be multiplied over and over again, leading the writer of Ecclesiastes to proclaim, "Vanity of vanities! All is vanity" (Eccl. 1:2).

So why should we not object to all this? What is the sense of making a world where two people could begin such a downward spiral? We in turn will have to trust in God and not pretend that we could have done things better. The biblical worldview is one in which God sets up the world in a particular way for his good purposes. First of all, throughout the pages of Scripture we are reminded that evil thoughts, words, and deeds are entirely our own responsibility. Only rarely is the connection with Adam made, though it is made. Interestingly, the apostle Paul in the book of Romans spends four chapters on human sinfulness and the need for grace before he even addresses the issue of Adam's relationship to humanity (Rom. 5:12-21). Whatever the relationship may be between Adam and his progeny, that does not get us off the hook as sinners fully accountable for our sin.

Second, we would be unwise, to say the least, to accuse God of having placed all human beings in an unfair relationship to their head. There is beauty and solidarity in such a kinship. There is real community and real fellowship in the human race. Often, philosophers and politicians search for a key to human cohesion. Well, here it is. If we don't like it, the challenge is to find a better alternative—but we cannot (Acts 17:26-27).

Third, why did the Lord not choose someone he knew would not disobey and create such havoc? We would be on thin ice to imagine that had God chosen some other covenant head besides Adam, he would have done a better job. Yet behind this question lies another, one that brings us closer to ultimate mysteries that are unsolvable by finite human beings: why did God create such a world, when he knew things would go wrong? We simply don't know, really. Somehow it was worthwhile to him. To say more puts us in danger of justifying evil, but of course, evil has no justification. If we say, "I know why God did this," then any reason we surmise could become an excuse.

There is more to say. God chose Adam, and he loved Adam and Eve. He gave them a noble task. They failed. But God did not leave them, or us, alone. Rather, he provided a way out, a costly solution, through his Son, Jesus Christ. As a result, then, our solidarity with Adam has been replaced. By a new solidarity with Jesus Christ (the second man, the last Adam), who is the covenant head of redeemed humanity, believers may be restored and may accomplish what our first parents failed to do (Rom. 5:15, 18–19, 21; 1 Cor. 15:45–49). In Christ, we may pass the test that Adam failed, because Christ passed it on our behalf. In fact, his test was far more difficult than that of Adam, because he faced it every day and ultimately had to pass the test of death itself. He then simply gave us the gift of his acquired righteousness for the asking (Rom. 3:21–26). Justification (acquittal from guilt) is by faith alone.

Having promised our first parents that despite their sin a fierce battle would be waged between the forces of evil (the seed of the serpent) and the forces of good (the seed of the woman), culminating in the triumph of good over evil, God has now won the victory (Gen. 3:15). Jesus would indeed crush the head of the serpent, though in the process he would become seriously damaged: he would die. But then he would be raised up in victory. Believers will be raised up as well, and sin, disease, and all sorrow will be gone. As the hymn puts it, "The strife is o'er, the battle done; the victory of life is won; the song of triumph has begun. Alleluia!"[2]

This is the story of the world according to the Bible. It is a profound story, one that is simple but deep and wide. For years, scientists and philosophers accepted the broad contours of this story and saw no particular conflict between the biblical account and their work. This has changed in the recent past, as we will see.

Before we move on

+ What were the consequences of Adam and Eve's failure and disobedience? Who is responsible for the existence of evil in this world?

+ What questions does the author raise here? What considerations must we take into account as we seek to answer these questions? Do you find the author's answers helpful? Why or why not?

+ What did God promise Adam and Eve? Why would he make this promise? What did his promise entail for him?

IS GOD IN CONTROL?

Evil came into the world through human disobedience. But that does not quite answer the question of God's relation to evil. Here we must proceed carefully. If we say that God simply created us with the capacity to choose and stood back to watch how things might unfold, we abandon any thought of his being all-powerful. An all-powerful God, one who ordains all things, does not stand back; he must somehow be in control of all things, including the forces of evil. Conversely, if we say that God causes evil to enter the world in a direct manner, we then deny human responsibility and make God a puppeteer, not the loving Father of mankind. Indeed, we become determinists, leaving no place for free agency.

What, then, is the answer? Above all, nothing must be posited that removes God's power. When God deals with history or with human life, he does not give up any of his sovereignty. When the New Testament tells us that Christ did not "count equality with God a thing to be grasped, but made himself nothing," it is not referring to Christ's being (Phil. 2:6–7). The second person of the Trinity cannot ever become less than God. This text, and others

15

like it, is referring to his act of becoming human, his condescension. The second person did not remove from his deity when he became a man. He added to it, but did not subtract from it. Only by becoming a man could Christ be subjected to pain, suffering, and mortality. We have here a high mystery. How can God remain God and yet take on properties that are decidedly un-Godlike?

Without becoming too technical, let me introduce two terms that will help to guide us through this issue. The first is *metaphysical*. It derives from the term *metaphysics*, addressing the question of what is there and what it is like. When we refer to God's being, we are doing metaphysics. We may say of God that he is immutable, unchangeable, always omnipotent, always good. Those are his metaphysical qualities. The second helpful term is *covenantal*. It derives from the term *covenant*, mentioned above, meaning an arrangement whereby God (in this case) enters into a special relationship with human beings. A covenantal arrangement is one in which God declares the terms of that relationship, both in its fundamental nature and in its requirements. In the first instance, God entered into a covenant relationship with his creation. When he created Adam and Eve, he entered into what is sometimes called a *covenant of works*—that is, he could require good works of Adam and Eve and put them through the test that we have mentioned above. When they failed, he then made a different covenant with humanity, known as the *covenant of grace* (he was certainly not obliged to do that; it was an act of undeserved mercy). This covenant has several administrations. From the earliest days right through to the new covenant, God saves his people by grace. Among others, Noah knew this covenant, as well as Abraham, David, and finally Jesus Christ, on our behalf (see Gen. 6:18; 17:7; 2 Chron 13:5; 14:7; Ps. 105:8; Heb. 9:15). This covenant of grace requires a Mediator, Jesus Christ, who secures our relationship with God through his death and resurrection (Heb. 12:24; 13:20).

BEFORE WE MOVE ON

+ What does *metaphysical* mean? Why is the question of God's relationship to evil a metaphysical question?

+ What does *covenantal* mean? What two covenants did God enter into with Adam and Eve? Who else was included in the second covenant?

By introducing these technical terms, we do not mean to detract from the wonder of the gospel or from the marvel of God's love. Indeed, because of this covenantal arrangement, God is able to call us his children: "See what kind of love the Father has given to us, that we should be called children of God; and so we are" (1 John 3:1). Nevertheless, these concepts will help us with our major task of discovering where evil ultimately comes from. Because what we want to arrive at is this: God can never change metaphysically, yet he can add covenantal qualities to himself in his relation with his creatures. Thus, when we consider the problem of evil, we may say that God has from all eternity ordained what will come to pass. If that could change, he would have to modify his being—change metaphysically. Which is impossible. Yet at the same time, he has made a world in which everything has meaning, everything is significant. Human beings have been given significant choices to make, resulting in real consequences. God can allow this because he has entered into a covenant relationship with the world and with human beings.

We still have a mystery here, because how can God, who is purer than to look upon evil, be somehow responsible for its entry into the world? Perhaps the best we can do is to deny some of the conclusions to which human reason might lead us if we did not have the light of revelation. By his "ordaining" everything, we cannot mean that God "is guilty for" some things. Here is how the Westminster Confession of Faith 3.1 puts it:

> God from all eternity did, by the most wise and holy counsel of his own will, freely and unchangeably ordain whatsoever comes to pass: yet so, as thereby neither is God the author of sin, nor is violence offered to the will of the creatures, nor is the liberty or contingency of second causes taken away, but rather established.

Notice the intricate wisdom of this declaration. Following so many clear affirmations in Scripture, the statement asserts God's sovereignty in the strongest possible terms. He decides absolutely everything from all eternity, by his own unconstrained will, unchangeably. And then, a marvelous colon. "Yet so," it goes on to say, denying what our unaided reason might be tempted to conclude (that God is the "author" of sin—authorship here equating to being accountable, responsible, or even guilty for sin). Not only so, but this kind of sovereignty does not violate the sovereignty of the creature. Nor does it violate what is called "second causes"—such things as rain for crops, food for survival, and the proper use of human reason to solve problems. Indeed, this kind of sovereignty makes such a world of significance possible. It makes possible a world that can rebel against its Maker.

Going back to our distinction, we can say that metaphysically, God ordains everything from all eternity, even the presence of evil in his world. But covenantally, he abhors evil and could eradicate it only by the costly death of his own beloved Son. If we may put it this way, there are two kinds of causes in the universe: the direct cause, whereby God decrees it and it comes to pass; and the secondary cause, whereby God respects the rules of his creation, including the freedom of his human creatures. Here is how Christian philosopher K. Scott Oliphint elegantly puts it:

> The fact that God himself takes on covenantal properties, properties that are not essential to him, but that nevertheless serve to characterize him, is the central focus of the good news of Scripture. It defines *the* good news for us—the news that God has come in the flesh and has, as God in the flesh, accomplished salvation for sinners. This is the preeminent truth of Scripture. It *is* the covenant, and it defines what we mean by covenant. In creating, God has "come down"; he has taken on that which is foreign to his essential being in order to relate to that which is essentially different from him.[3]

While such clarifications certainly do not solve all the problems, we can nevertheless go a little beyond just calling the entrance of evil into the world a pure mystery. Human beings, beginning with Adam, are responsible for it, and they will be called to account for their decisions. This is the reality of the covenant. Yet God is ultimately the one who decides all things, including the presence of evil—a presence for which he is nevertheless not culpable. And best of all, God, in his mercy, has provided an extraordinary solution to the problem of evil: by taking on human nature, obeying where we failed to obey, and suffering where we deserved to suffer. That is the gospel!

BEFORE WE MOVE ON

+ Which quality of God must we be very careful not to reduce as we do metaphysics? What tension does this lead to when we consider evil?

+ How does this answer maintain human responsibility for sin?

✦ What does it mean to say that God "takes on covenantal properties"? How has he done so in history? How is this good news—in fact, *the* good news?

A WORD ABOUT SCIENCE

One of the great challenges of our day is trying to see how this biblical account that we have been describing fits the data we can observe from the world around us. While it is not our purpose to write a treatise on Christian faith and science, a few observations are in order. Here is a safe presupposition: the same God who gave us the Bible also created the world. If there are gaps or unsolved problems in relating the two, that is because of our limitations, not because there are any fundamental contradictions. As Francis Bacon (1561–1626) once put it, the same God who gave us the "book of his Word" also gave us the "book of nature."[4]

Only in relatively recent times have many scientists called into question the worldview described above. Quite the opposite was the case in the centuries before the Enlightenment. Medieval thinkers engaged in what we now call *science* because they believed that God was a God of order. During the Reformation, John Calvin (1509–64) said that the natural light God provided helped men to "discern the truth about nature," and that the Scriptures helped to make that discernment even stronger, as a pair of eyeglasses helps the sight.[5] Calvin's student Lambert Daneau (1535–90) wrote that pagan learning was deficient for morality and science, but that Christians, working with both general and special revelation, could know the motion of the planets, the foundations of the world, and the "top of the heavens."[6]

You will find scientists in the seventeenth century who believed their call was to help humanity return to the way Adam and Eve would have lived in the garden of Eden. One of the most remarkable of such scholars was Johann Heinrich Alsted (1588–1638), a professor at Herborn Academy in Germany, who published a widely read encyclopedia of knowledge (*Encyclopaedia* [1630]). It was his conviction that philosophy and all the legitimate disciplines (the term *science* was not yet in use) served for the "instauration" of the image of God, damaged by the fall.[7] Many of the pioneers of modern science, household names, were consciously trying to find the order of the universe because they believed that God was a God of order. The list includes Copernicus, Galileo, Kepler, Newton, Pascal, Boyle, and numerous others.

Things began to change in the seventeenth century and on into the eighteenth. What basically occurred was an increasing belief that what we have called *second causes* are in fact primary causes. To make a long story short, by the time of David Hume (1711–76), many skeptics were doubting the direct role of God in making the world or governing it. Some, such as the so-called deists, thought that God had made the world and that perhaps we could know him by intuition, but that he could not be clearly perceived in the world. Indeed, deists believed that God never interfered with the world's ongoing processes—that only natural laws were necessary for its daily functions. Eventually they began to doubt that Jesus Christ could have come into the world from heaven to live and die on behalf of a particular people, for that would have been something unworthy of a fair-minded Creator. Deists were generally not atheists. As one scholar described them, deists were "rationalists with a nostalgia for religion."[8] That is, they were basically skeptics, yet they did not want to go down the slippery slope to atheism.

In this atmosphere a century later, Charles Darwin (1809–82) and his followers went so far as to offer plausible alternative explanations for the creation of the world and the "fall" into evil. Gradually throughout his life Darwin became less and less convinced that a God active in the creation was necessary. He argued that if God had made the world uniform, he did not really need to interact with it. The basic outlook that Darwin articulated, called the theory of *evolution*, was that species evolved and adapted to their environs by *natural selection*. Just as it is happening today, he thought, it has been happening for a long time. What he meant is that living things reproduce more readily, and thus survive better, when they are more fit for their places of habitation. Such a process explained the extraordinary diversity of plants and animals—a law, Darwin claimed. Eventually Darwin came to believe that man was directly related to animals, particularly to the apes.

Darwin never lost his faith in a creator God altogether. But he lost the conviction that the Bible was reliable and that Jesus Christ was the Son of God. He commented that while earlier he could look at a beautiful waterfall in Brazil and see the handiwork of God, now it was just a natural phenomenon. Most especially, Darwin was troubled by the violence in nature and thought that if God were somehow involved in the world's affairs, it could be only indirectly, since things were so awry. Darwin's theories appeared to be finally vindicated in the 1950s with the appearance of *Neo-Darwinism*, a name given to the view that genetics are the primary cause of adaptation. Things evolve through mutations, which are then inherited in subsequent generations.[9] Many scientists today do not accept a purely Darwinian theory, but they still believe that evolution, and particularly genetics, provides all the explanation we need for the development of life, including human life.

How do evolutionists explain the origins of evil? Darwin himself wrote to fellow scientist Asa Gray, "I own that I cannot see as plainly as others do, and as I should wish to do, evidence of design and beneficence on all sides of us. There seems to me too much misery in the world." He could cite several examples. One of them was a wasp that lives inside a caterpillar, gradually eating its host until it is dead. "I cannot persuade myself that a beneficent and omnipotent God would have designedly created the ichneumonidae [parasitic wasps] with the express intention of their feeding within the living bodies of caterpillars, or that a cat should play with mice."[10]

Christians ought to have strong sympathies with Darwin's sensitivity. Not everything in nature seems well designed by a beneficent God. Where does death come from? What about animal violence? As we have seen, human death is explained in Scripture as a result of rebellion against God. So how does this fit with scientific observation? For materialistic science, human death is just there. For many, the idea of good and evil is merely a human construct. If there is no God, then why trouble ourselves about death, cruelty, and the like? Richard Dawkins, one of the more outspoken of the so-called new atheists, says quite baldly, "The universe we observe has precisely the properties we should expect if there is at bottom no design, no purpose, no evil and no good, nothing but pointless indifference."[11] The great difficulty with Dawkins's position is that throughout his work he actually does identify certain activities as evil. For example, he considers raising a child in the Christian faith to be an evil worse than child abuse.[12] He builds a sort of secular morality based on his own ten commandments. Is this a slip of the pen, or is something deeper going on? There is something far deeper. Whether he acknowledges it or not, Richard Dawkins is one of God's image-bearers, and he is living in the world that God has made, the world in which God sets the contours of good and evil.

Darwin, for me, is the more admirable figure. He cried out for justice. He was deeply troubled about evil, including human death. He hoped evolutionary theory would provide some kind of answer. But could it do that? "Although Darwin's gritty world cried out for justice, his evolution would grant none, for it would call back that there was no injustice in the first place."[13] Eventually, though, Darwin tried to argue that the evolutionary process actually produced a kind of morality. Survival of the fittest can explain faith and ethics. We need religion and we need morality at least to be able to navigate the rough waters of the world, much as the monkey learns to fear the snake, he said. But does this kind of survival tactic really provide an acceptable basis for morality? And above all, does it give us reasons to be outraged at evil? The attempt is bold, but unsuccessful.

In the end, a purely materialistic version of evolutionary theory is simply incapable of explaining why we are repulsed at the phenomenon of human death. Indeed, it is incapable of naming death and suffering evil. It certainly cannot help us decide how evil got into the world.

Before we move on

+ What did early Western scientists believe about God? How did this mind-set shift in the 1600s and 1700s? How did deists further develop this new mind-set? How did Darwin do so?

+ How can we be sympathetic to Darwin's reaction to the violence in nature? Why might we have less sympathy for Dawkins's secular morality? Can a materialistic worldview take evil into account at all? Why or why not?

DEATH BEFORE THE FALL?

A word is in order here to further define what we mean by *evil*. Is every form of hostility, or what we perceive to be cruel, contrary to God's beneficence? Is every form of violence, including the death of plants and animals, a result of the fall? The Bible does teach that the fall of mankind affected nature. That is clear from God's terrible words to Adam right after he had sinned: "cursed is the ground because of you" (Gen. 3:17). There is a good deal of teaching on this relationship. Because of the people's rebellion, God kindles a fire that burns to the depths of Sheol and devours the earth and its increase. Disasters, hunger, disease—all of these come from God's displeasure (Deut. 32:22ff.).

And yet does that mean that all death is the result of the fall? Are the deaths of plants, or even animals, something necessarily evil? Are all beasts of prey evildoers? Admittedly we don't like to see predators stalking, killing, and then devouring their victims. We even hate it when our pets die. But are we informed by biblical sensitivities or by a more romantic view of a peaceful and tranquil nature, so popular and yet perhaps untrue?

A number of portions of Scripture describe God as taming the wild forces in the creation. Even a creation that is good can have untamed features. In his admonition to Job, the Lord asks him whether he could, like God, have shut the sea with doors, or have seen the gates of deep darkness (Job 38:8, 17). He further asks him whether he can hunt the prey of the lion, or provide for the young raven (38:39–41). Some animals are selfish, like the ostrich, others mighty, like the horse (39:13ff.). The natural world, in the biblical view, is a place of both generosity and violence. God may cause grass to grow for livestock, and plants for man to cultivate for food (Ps. 104:14). But he also makes the darkness, a time when beasts of the forest creep about. Young lions roar for their prey, seeking their food from God (vv. 20–21). If God hides his face, the animals are dismayed, and eventually they die (v. 29). Is the creation really a safe and peaceful place, made violent only by the fall? When Paul tells us that creation has been subject to bondage and decay, he does not say why or when it started (Rom. 8:21). He does say "until now" (v. 22), but he does not say from when. The garden of Eden was a wonderful place, but it was not yet the place of consummate bliss, the place of eternal life. The "glory" that is to be revealed is still to come. So there could have been death in various places, without any implications of God's authorship of evil. Not human death, but death nevertheless.

For now, the creation groans and is anything but a safe and peaceful place. Some of that groaning may be due to the fall. But some of it is surely from the yet-untamed portion of the creation, a creation that even from the beginning longed for full glory. There is real hope, the certainty that one day there will be glory. And we cannot be sure that such glory will altogether exclude the death of plants and animals. We simply do not know. We do have indications that things will be tranquil and not violent. A number of places in the Bible suggest that all will be peaceful: "The wolf shall dwell with the lamb, and the leopard shall lie down with the young goat . . . . The nursing child shall play over the hole of the cobra" (Isa. 11:6–8). These may be symbolic images, although they may be literal as well.

To be sure, *human* death was a result of the fall. God told Adam and Eve that they would die if they took of the fruit of the forbidden tree. And while they did not die physically the moment they transgressed, they died spiritually. And then eventually they did die physically, as does every human being since (with the miraculous exceptions of a very few, such as Enoch and Elijah). But why, then, should animals have to die? We don't know altogether. For Darwin, it was so that the fittest would survive and thus achieve progress. Yet for him, God seemed very distant from such a process. But the Bible gives us a very different picture of the relation between man and beast. Adam gave names to the animals (Gen. 2:20). He was to rule over the beasts as well as vegetation, and to subdue them and enjoy them (1:28–29).

Perhaps death in the plant and animal realms is there to demonstrate to people what death is. Psalm 49:12 states, "Man in his pomp will not remain; he is like the beasts that perish." Perhaps death in the vegetable and animal worlds shows us what life and death are all about. Sinful people are like the beasts, who die, Ecclesiastes tells us (3:18–22), although the reason for human death is "wickedness" (v. 16).

We can say a bit more. The apostle Paul turns the reality of death in the natural world into an argument for the resurrection. As he puts it, "What you sow does not come to life unless it dies. . . . What is sown is perishable, what is raised is imperishable" (1 Cor. 15:36, 42). Then he makes the analogy with our natural body and our resurrection body. It gets complicated, but basically he is telling us that the first humanity was earthly, made from the dust, whereas redeemed humanity is heavenly, joined to "the man of heaven," Jesus Christ (vv. 47–49). So if not all death is evil or caused by the fall, death in the natural realm does signify the temporary, the first installment. We can look forward to the permanent, the final chapter, the new heavens and new earth, where there is no death.

Before we move on

+ What do we know for sure was a result of the fall? What does this mean for other potentially disturbing events in nature? What might these things teach us about death and evil?

A CALL FOR MODESTY

Our appeal to mystery as we looked into the matter of God's role in the origins of evil should certainly be matched by a similar call to humility when examining the world scientifically. New studies are coming out all the time that call into serious question some of the doctrines of evolution, including Neo-Darwinism.[14] It would be a shame to invest in a theory about origins that might sound plausible but that is due for serious criticism and even refutation. For the moment, there are many questions about the validity of theories once thought to be airtight.

Where does this leave us? In the first place, it is always safe to return to Scripture, which, though not a modern scientific text to be sure, is God's authoritative revelation to his creatures. In the Bible we will find all we need in order to live in God's world. While we could wish that this book gave us more detailed information about the mechanics of creation and the origins of mankind, it gives us what we need to know. And it gives us the exciting vocation to explore God's world and uncover its riches. In other words, it gives us a mandate to do the work of scientific research, as long as we do it for the glory of God and not to aggrandize human rationality.

Despite all the precautions that we have laid out here, it would be wrong to think that Christians should somehow stay out of the sciences. To the contrary, if we believe that we have a responsibility to work against the fall and to anticipate the world to come, then not only *may* we do science, but we *must* engage in it and its first cousin, technology. What a privilege it is to explore God's world, to identify the sources of evil, and then to work against evil by using the wisdom and knowledge that God has given us. "Do you not know," asks Paul, "that the saints will judge the world?" (1 Cor. 6:2). We have the great privilege of understanding the world and learning how it works. We can discern wrong paths and guide our fellow humans down the right path. "Test everything; hold fast what is good. Abstain from every form of evil" (1 Thess. 5:21–22). What a marvelous calling.

How did evil come into the world? The Bible gives us the primary information we need to work with. And scientific observation comes to serve us and help us to ask key questions about God's creation and how things went wrong. Such questions take us back to the Bible. We need both special revelation and general revelation to develop the kind of knowledge needed to navigate in this world and to understand God's ways.[15]

IN CONCLUSION

✢ What is evil?

✢ How did evil come into the world?

✢ How are humans responsible for evil? How is God *not*?

✢ What would be absent from a perfect world? What might still be present?

✢ What can we do about evil in the world?

NOTES

1. The title of a marvelous book on the subject of evil by Cornelius Plantinga, *Not the Way It's Supposed to Be: A Breviary of Sin* (Grand Rapids: Eerdmans, 1995).

2. "The Strife Is O'er, the Battle Done," Latin hymn, trans. Francis Pott, 1861.

3. K. Scott Oliphint, *Reasons for Faith: Philosophy in the Service of Theology* (Phillipsburg, NJ: P&R Publishing, 2006), 259.

4. Francis Bacon, *The Great Instauration and the Novum Organum* (1620; repr., Whitefish, MT: Kessinger Publications, 2010), 1:71, 241.

5. *Institutes of the Christian Religion*, 1.6.1; 1.14.1.

6. *The Wonderful Workmanship of the World* (London, 1578), fol. 4v., available online at http://books.google.com/books?id=3lkYAAAAYAAJ.

7. See Howard Hotson, *Johann Heinrich Alston, 1588–1638: Between Renaissance, Reformation and Universal Reform* (New York: Oxford University Press, 2000), 70–74.

8. M. Paul Hazard, quoted in Basil Willey, *The Eighteenth Century Background*, 3rd ed. (Boston: Beacon Press, 1964), 11.

9. In fact, there are numerous problems with the genetic evidence for evolution. Mathematicians generally do not accept the possibility of such vast changes in the genome over a relatively short period.

10. Letter from Charles Darwin to Asa Gray, May 22, 1860; quoted in Nancy H. Frankenberry, ed., *The Faith of Scientists in Their Own Words* (Princeton: Princeton University Press, 2008), 129.

11. Richard Dawkins, *River out of Eden* (New York: Basic Books, 1996), 132.

12. Richard Dawkins, *The God Delusion* (New York: Mariner Books, 2008), 354.

13. Cornelius G. Hunter, *Darwin's God: Evolution and the Problem of Evil* (Grand Rapids: Brazos Press, 2001), 154.

14. See, for example, Stephen C. Meyer, Paul A. Nelson, and Jonathan Moneymaker, *Explore Evolution: The Arguments for and against Neo-Darwinism* (Melbourne: Hill House, 2009). Critics of Neo-Darwinism are not necessarily believers. See atheist Thomas Nagel's *Mind and Cosmos: Why the Materialist Neo-Darwinian Conception of Nature Is Almost Certainly False* (New York: Oxford University Press, 2012).

15. For a helpful treatment of the relation between general and special revelation, see Cornelius Van Til, "Nature and Scripture," in *The Infallible Word*, ed. Paul Woolley (Phillipsburg, NJ: P&R Publishing, 2003), 263–301.